The Contract

Never forget what your grandmothers did for you!

Steve Levi

Master of the Impossible Crime
Author Masterminds Charter Member

Illustrator Amanda Saxton

PUBLICATION CONSULTANTS
We Believe In The Power Of Authors

PO Box 221974 Anchorage, Alaska 99522-1974

books@publicationconsultants.com—www.publicationconsultants.com

ISBN 978-1-59433-972-1
eBook ISBN 978-1-59433-973-8

Alaska Historical
Publication Association

The Contract is published in part by grants from the
Puffin Foundation, West LTD, Alaska Historical
Publication Association, and The Usibelli Foundation.

Manufactured in the United States of America.

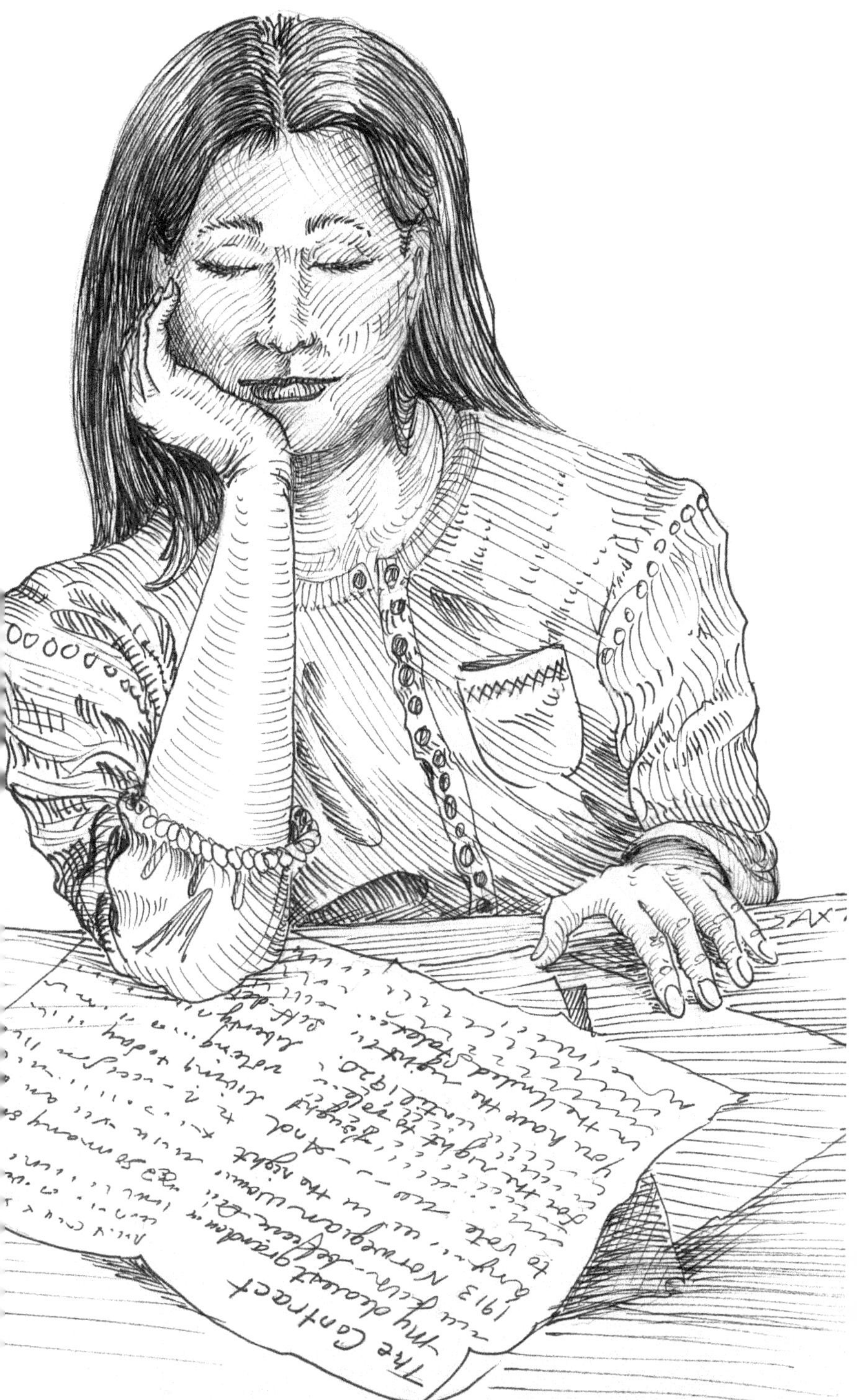
The Contract

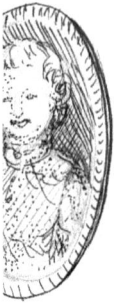

Jenny sat pouting alone in her room
at her cosmetic table dabbing perfume;
a dot on her ankle and one on her wrist,
flicking some in her hair the scent to assist
her inspired version of a modern-day woman
of charm and intrigue and dash of homespun.

Lipstick and hair glow with peaches-and-cream
complexion assistance made her skin gleam.
She counted the strokes as she brushed her blond hair
checking the roots for hints of brown there.
Then she squeezed into her bra and tightened her belt
for the hourglass figure to make the boys melt.

Her book bag in hand she descended the stairs
to the kitchen and mother cooking with care
the meal a young lady needed for strength
for classes and boys and peer pressure ranks.
She settled herself on the edge of a chair
expressing her anguish with no venom spared.

"Momma," she said still in a rage,
"it seems some of the boys have it all made.
They play all the sports and date the whole field
looking for any girl who will yield
to seductive phrases mixed with muscle and smiles
with cash and hot cars all to beguile

"giddy girls with the brains of an oyster or clam
who believe that success is getting a man
whose word is his honor and honor his word
knowing full well that both are absurd.
Some boys fiddle in class and disdain the text books,
they don't study for tests and give such awful looks

"when someone suggests that they study a bit.
Once out of school their fortunes won't hit
the shoals of the world where knowledge arcane
determines one's speed up the food chain.
The curse of it all, and I know this to be true,
is that being a man is a hallowed virtue;

"they get the good job, the perks and the fame
and rely for promotion on their fathers' names.
They're doctors and lawyers and teachers and priests
while we have to settle for clerical seats.
What chance do we have when laden with child
but to give up our jobs with only a smile?

"It's unfair, it's unreal, it's uncouth, it's obscene
that I have to struggle in school only to glean
the lowest of jobs because the men have the rest
and my chances of fortune and fame, at best:
to be some husband's nanny to children enchained
and depend on his salary instead of my brain.

*"So I have to spend time with lipstick and perfume
for the best I can do is to snare a bridegroom
and vicariously live from his successes and hope
while I'm up to my elbows in diapers and soap.
I don't need a degree; I need a sexual change
if I want a career that leads to money and fame."*

"Her mother in bathrobe did not a sound make
as she stood poking her spatula into hot cakes
that sizzled and plumped in the cast iron pan.
When the dough crusted to a succulent tan
she expertly flipped the flapjacks with ease
then looked up at her daughter with a visage displeased.

She pointed the spatula toward Jenny with care
and waggled it back and forth in the air,
*"You, my dear Jenny, are an ignorant imp
with the outlook of a woman who's looking to pimp
her future for myths she's burned into her head
rather than use common sense instead of her bed.*

*"Life isn't easy and comes without directions
so the choices you make must be made with inspections
for once in a rut of your life's occupation
your career will feel more like self-flagellation.
Your future's design is made 'tween your ears
not your breasts that will sag as you pick up years.*

"Let me tell you a story that you've never heard
about your grandmother of whom you've not heard a word.
In her day she was quite a nymphet
who metamorphosed into suffragette
because she was expected to raise up a brood
rather than work as a lawyer and earn her own food.

"She was born, I admit, with a spoon in her mouth,
silver-plated it was, let me leave you no doubt.
She came not from rich stock but was sturdy of worth
growing up in a city where sidewalks were dirt.
She worked as a seamstress until her fingertips bled
then decided there were better ways to earn her own bread.

"On evening and weekends she went to Night School
where 'up and out' was the ongoing rule.
She plowed her way upward to a college degree
then continued the climb to an LLD.
She spent a lifetime of sweat of both brow and brain
to achieve what most women then thought was in vain.

"The greatest of shock came when with her degree
she could not get a job because of the disease
known as "male chauvinism for a woman with brains"
was nothing more than a murderess with a cleaver bloodstained.
So she wandered the streets with her degree in her hand
caught between common labor and needing a man.

"No one wanted a lawyer who worked in a dress
or a woman whose brains could be proven best,
they wanted a MAN, regardless his skill
and that, simply put, was the required skill.
There were many excuses, most of them lame
of why males were being hired but never the dames.

"And thus she was caught, your grandmother, Jenny
between being a woman with prospects not many
save finding a MAN and raising up children
the better half of them being young men
who would rule their own families just like a pasha
and repeat the same cycle ad nausea.

"But Grandma was not the most genteel of sorts
when it came to those whose IQ was well short
of room temperature or had a brain in perpetual freeze
'tween six inches of bone and viscous as cheese.
Her future, she knew, was in her own hands
and it was fight for her rights or marry a man.

"Once out on the streets and far from her home
she found in her plight she wasn't alone.
There were women from up town and down near the docks
who were tired of slavery to the homemaker stocks.
They wanted more than being chained to their hearth
but careers and professions in business and art

"So they gathered in groups, in klatches and dens
in neighborhood halls and farmer's pig pens,
in the rain and the snow and the wind and the mud
where their mutual passion made them thicker than blood
for the right to explore their potential and yearnings
instead of the chains of what their husband was earning.

VOTE
TO WIN
FREEDOM
FOR
WOMEN

"They gathered on sidewalks and assembled in parks
loitered on street corners with sandwich placards
with pamphlets and leaflets and buttons and cards
they bombarded old Boston with political charge
then to New York, LA and all in between
from ocean to ocean and both portside and beam.

"They discovered allies in the most unlikely of places
in tenement houses and rural farm spaces
for women of all ages, religions and fervor
hungered for rights that had been lost in the fever
of Westward expansion where women stayed home
while the men with the oxen turned over the loam.

"But now that the nation had grown and matured
the role of the woman had become immured
in the belief that the best which she could offer
was children and cocktails and bed companion softer
than burlap for pillow and a blanket for bed
on the range moving cattle of hundreds of head.

"Their numbers grew stronger their marches grew longer
as more and more women did wake up and conjure
they could exorcise the male chauvinist beast
of the belief that women were nothing more than treats
destined for duty in kitchens and beds
seductive of body but with vacuous heads."

Rolling her eyes in anguish and angst
Jenny said with frustration, *"For the lecture, Mom, thanks,*
but I've heard of the struggle to get women the vote
of Stanton and Sanger and the women of note
but grandma was born in 1923
well after after the passage of Amendment 19!"

"BINGO!" said Mom clearing her throat,
"but there's more to this story then winning the vote.
It's the ongoing struggle for equality
in the home on the job site in court and settee,
for the forces against us never take off a night
and all people must battle to maintain their rights --

"besides, my young friend, the stories you've heard
are those of your GREAT grandma, a tough campaigning bird
who fought for YOUR rights with Stanton and Sanger
walking the streets in the face of men's anger,
the demands of women were not just getting the vote
but giving you the option of a career of note.

"The problem with youth is they diddle in school
and ignore the most basic of history's rules:
you have only the rights for which you will fight
and you must join up with others to add to your might.
You make your own luck; you choose your own party,
pay your own dues and form your own army.

"It's easy to say that someone is blessed
because of more money than all of the rest
but that's an error, a lie and red herring
for anyone can make cash and be born with good bearing
but a home run, as they say in the bull pen,
is that which divides the boys from the men.

"It was your GREAT grandma that fought for the vote
and on her deathbed my mother took oath
that the fight for the rights of women and men
would be the same regardless of which children
were raised in the household or sent off to school;
all would be treated the same was the new rule.

"The 19th Amendment was merely Step One,
the start of a race that will never be won
as long as young women give up the game
because it's too easy to just change your name.
There is never an end to the struggle for rights
for you have only those for which you will fight.

"The 19th Amendment was nothing more
than a starting gun that opened the door
and changed the word 'fairness' from a rallying call
to a quest for good jobs Winter, Summer and Fall
and men now understood women as a perennial flood
in the quest for careers both squalid and good.

"*Most men had assumed that after the vote
women would retreat to the kitchen leaving banknotes
to be earned by their husbands – but what a shock
when the women demanded their right to buy stock!
with money they'd earned from professional careers
they chose based on IQs not their brassieres.*

"Blue collar, white collar, labor and boss,
bean counter, seamstress and fish mongeress,
women flooded the job market from New York to LA,
small cities, farm towns and in urban forays
they demanded their due in the work of the nation
and set off a Civil Rights Revolution.

"The press it was brutal and the spectators cruel
casting invectives and empty thread spools
crying "Get back to the kitchen! Leave working to men!
You are needed at home by your snot-nosed children!"
Lampooned in the papers and harassed by their peers
women who worked earned nothing but sneers.

"Though life is unfair it does have its tools
and one is that righteousness, in the end rules,
in that rainstorm of insults was planted a seed
that rooted deep in soil of the American dream
for in this land of the red, white and blue
all have the same chance, men, Blacks and Jews.

"You are only as smart as your schooling is
and when you stop thinking that's the end of the biz,
you become frozen in amber in whatever age
it was when you last turned a book's page
and the faster the world passes you by
the stronger you cling to conservative ties.

"Now the greatest of enemies you'll ever meet
are those who have the most to lose in market or street.
I'm not talking about men who work for their bread
but of the women who prefer to stay home in bed
for like the flow of water in rivers and creeks
it is easier to loaf than to struggle to meet

car payments and rent and write checks that don't bounce
while balancing carbs and fats by the ounce.
The greatest of foe is she from within
the ranks of those whom you take for friends.
This enemy's young, old, fat and thin
and cares only for what's in it for them.

"Every noble endeavor in the end becomes
nothing more than a racket to which one succumbs.
Playing the odds in the hope of a gain
is a fool's paradise and playing a game
that will end you up worse than when you began
and like poker and craps is nothing more than a scam.

"I tell you this, Jenny, for growing in ranks
are women who believe that their sex outranks
the work that they do and the reports they submit
and make up for their errors with law suits and writs.
No one is a victim, those who tell you to quit
want you to join them in the ranks of dimwits.

"Life is not fair; it gets all twisted and turned
as you grow ever older you will undoubtedly learn
that failure is personal and success comes at you with stealth
advertising brings riches but marketing wealth --
but of all that you earn and all that you owe
you will only earn that of which you sow.

"Success comes to those who are better or best
with run-of-the-mill people being the rest.
Those with any brains are scattered and few
and the rest of the workers don't have a clue;
from run-of-the-mill people comes run-of-the-mill work
and they'll never rise higher than cashier or clerk.

"A fool is the one who laughs rather than listen
and opportunities do not all with gold glisten.
Beware of your labels for an arrogant man
could be more aware of his true worth than
a man's who's a clone and knows his cost to the penny
for few know their true worth, and listen up, Jenny,

"we're all in this alone, both women and men,
and we all earn our own way with our brains and the pen
there is only one rule for those who want to survive
and that is to continue to strive
and if you want to be nothing more than a clone in the pack
don't expect more than a pat on the back.

"Never forget what your grandmothers did
while many of her friends only backslid;
she sacrificed then to give you a chance
to shoot for success by your own advance.
Your contract with those women was only a gift
Now it's up to you to take the gearshift."

As Jenny pondered what had been said
Mom flicked off the stove and bagged the cornbread.
Then she pulled off her robe and brushed off the crumbs
from her suit and silk stockings with nary a run
that she wore to the desk where she managed accounts
for Fortune Five Hundred home office amounts.

"The choice is yours, Jenny," Mom said at the front door
"Anyone can quit but success takes a lot more
of gumption and guts and the drive to succeed,
you have to be smart and choose work over greed.
Your grandmothers and I can do nothing more
It's up to you now for we've opened the door."

Jenny sat silent, alone at the nook,
and looked from the door to her bag of books.
She pondered the hopes her mother expressed
and weighed her own chances of achieving success.
The choice was hers now; Mom could do no more
than like grandma before, open the door.

I WANT TO BE A SUFFRAGETTE
Tune: "Give My Regards to Broadway"

I want to be a suffragette
to show my mommy I won't forget
that being a woman is something to be proud of
not anything to bow your head because of
so I want to a suffragette
to make my mommy proud.

I'm old enough to vote and hold a job
and a heck of a lot better than my brother Bob
I don't drink until midnight and sleep 'till noon
I'd be at work before the milk man's through
I've got the education and the skill to wow
so where are all the jobs for the women now!

I want to be a suffragette
to show my mommy I won't forget
that being a woman is something to be proud of
not anything to bow your head because of
so I want to a suffragette
to make my mommy proud.

Any man can get a job all he needs is pants
while women get the children and the marriage rants
I want a job that's more than an occupation
to build myself a well deserved reputation
I'm only unemployed because of my sex
But you ain't heard the last of me yet.

I want to be a suffragette
to show my mommy I won't forget
that being a woman is something to be proud of
not anything to bow your head because of
so I want to a suffragette
to make my mommy proud.

A crook can put his ballot in a voting box;
a drunk can hold a job as long as he wears socks
so why can't a woman with a law degree
work in a high class New York company?
Give me the chance and I'll show my stuff
'cause every gal deserves a chance to strut.

I want to be a suffragette
to show my mommy I won't forget
that being a woman is something to be proud of
not anything to bow your head because of
so I want to a suffragette
to make my mommy proud.

I got my education at the best of schools
graduated top dog didn't break any rules;
now I want my chance to earn my own bread
want a good job where I can hold up my head
I'm just as good as any guy
Hey, Mr. boss man, give me a try.

I want to be a suffragette
to show my mommy I won't forget
that being a woman is something to be proud of
not anything to bow your head because of
so I want to a suffragette
to make my mommy proud.

When I get older gonna have me some kids
Hope they're all girls, I won't fib
Send them off to school to get the best education
So they can lead women across the nation
Women are just as good as the guys
So come on America, give us a try.

THE LADIES'S ROOM UPSTAIRS
Tune: "Abdul Abulbul Amir"

The most elegant man in the ballroom
was stunning in black tux and tails,
and sported a maid on his forearm
with piercing black eyes and hair pale.

Those in the know recognized her
though they couldn't remember her name;
all they knew was she was an accountant
at Fitzpatrick, Smithson and James.

Yes, she was an accountant
the best, in fact, at the firm
but since she was a lady
she needed a man on her stern.

A lion does its best business
at the watering hole
amid the bellows and belches
as the beasts in the water roll.

So she was drawn to the parties
where the business leads were to be had
but she needed a man for admittance
and could hardly depend on her dad.

She chose a man most appealing
a stud horse to distract the horde
an appropriate escort for a lady
who would race but would never score.

She wanted a seat in the boardroom
in one of the soft leather chairs
but the boardroom had only one toilet
and the ladies room was located down stairs.

She made the firm lots of money
she made it without any shame
but stayed stuck in the accounting department
at Fitzpatrick, Smithson and James.

Thus is the tale of a sad lass
who was cursed for being a gal
but she got her revenge in the long run
by putting three daughters through Yale.

Now all three sit in the boardroom
despite the snickers of stares
at Fitzpatrick, Smithson and James.
and the ladies' room now is upstairs.

I'M NOT A BIRD IN A GILDED CAGE
Tune: "A Bird in a Gilded Cage"

I'm not a bird in a gilded cage
with time to preen and feather,
I'm a sales girl with acreage
and men who think they're my betters
who won't sell bonnets off the floor
or corsets off the rack,
to even talk to customers
sets them all aback.

I'm not a bird in a gilded cage;
I earn my pay each day.
I know which clothes are quite the rage
and what working girls will pay.
The men say that I'm lucky
to sell clothing off the rack
instead of sewing on buckles
or working on my back.

I'm not a bird in a gilded cage
and offers have I plenty
but I say now because a page
will be turned in 1920.
I'll not be stuck at the butter churn,
I'll be a brigadier
then the men can take their turn
selling bloomers and brassieres.